★ ★ ★ ★ ★

THE RESURRECTION OF
AUTHENTIC
MANHOOD

Restoring God's Original Design

GEORGE SAWYER

MY HEALTHY CHURCH®
Equipping Spirit-Empowered People

Published by My Healthy Church
1445 North Boonville Avenue
Springfield, Missouri 65802

Editor: Linda A. Schantz

ISBN: 978-1-62423-089-9

Printed in the United States of America

16 15 14 13 • 1 2 3 4 5 6 7 8

DEDICATION

My life has been unusually blessed. I've never had to look far to see authentic manhood. My father was one of the greatest Christian men I have ever known. There is no other man that I would consider dedicating a book on manhood to but him. I gratefully and humbly dedicate this book to George W. Sawyer, my father, my hero, my friend.

I pray that the lessons I learned from my father and the love I received from him can be passed on to my dear family and to a generation of men desperate for examples of true authentic manhood.

My father was a man's man. A World War II veteran, an entrepreneur, he founded his own construction company and built churches in the U.S. and foreign countries—many at his own expense. He loved God, his family, his church, and his pastor. His influence for Christ on his business partners, employees, and fellow church members was truly amazing. My father was a textbook example of the gift of giving.

My father went to heaven in March 2012. His legacy will live on through our family and the thousands of lives that he touched. Thank you, Dad, for modeling Christ for me every day of your life. Your faith and love fill every page of this book. When I grow up I want to be just like you.

This book is dedicated to my father but it is in honor of my wife, Phyllis. Thank you, Phyllis—for everything my father taught me, you have been with me as I learned to walk out these truths.

As we started a family and planted a church, you took every step with me. You are the kind of wife, mother, and woman that every man dreams of. You are beautiful, fearless, faithful, and godly. You have challenged me to grow in prayer and sacrificial giving. You listen to my biggest dreams and then go to work as only you can—and they happen! You have been there as I have grown into a man. You know my strengths and my weaknesses, and you just make me better. You are the wind beneath my wings. Our family and our church are better because of you. I love you.

Contents

FOREWORD

The plane was coming into the final approach to land in Tulsa, Oklahoma. While others were preparing for their departure, gearing up to jump out of their seats, grab their bags and go, my spirit was listening. I can only describe it as a deposit, a word of knowledge. I sensed God speaking to me three statements:

1. I want you to build a movement to resurrect authentic manhood.

2. Focus on a man's purpose, and he will cast off those things that restrain him.

3. *"The purposes of a man's heart are deep waters, but a man of understanding draws them out."*
   Proverbs 20:5

In the ordinary moment of a commute, God spoke to me.

I immediately had two follow-up questions.

"What are the purposes of a man?"

I thought I knew, but in reality, I had no real understanding of what God's original intention for man was.

My father did not raise me. I had no example of an authentic man in my life. Although God had blessed me with a wonderful wife and three children, I hadn't clearly defined authentic manhood for my own life.

So, I looked deeply into the verse that echoed in my spirit, *"The purposes of a man's heart are deep waters, but a man of understanding draws them out."*

The Hebrew word translated as "man" in that verse is *iysh*. It means *masculine; definitively male, as opposed to a female.* Proverbs 20:5 is clearly speaking of authentic manhood. The defined maleness of *iysh* can be categorized into five distinct purposes: Man has an adventurous spirit. He has an entrepreneurial drive. He is gallant in relationships. He is faithful in character, and he is philanthropic in cause (desiring to leave a legacy).

As I speak to men around the world these five purposes resonate within them—not because we are attempting to make them something they are not, but because we are speaking clearly to what they already are. When men hear about authentic manhood, they lean forward into a ready stance—ready for action, ready to change.

I asked God my second follow-up question.

"How do you build a movement?"

Building a movement is very different than building a company or a ministry. Building a movement requires a completely different mindset. A movement is birthed out of the actions of people who influence culture and communicate a shared ideology for determined results. The process is fourfold: build your platform, expand your reach, gather your tribe, and change the culture.

After receiving this challenge from God, I shared what I had heard with a few trusted family members and friends. I believe it's always wise to take a few days to muse over any message and check it out. With one accord it was confirmed that I had heard from God.

My next step was to invite a small group of ministers and businessmen to a gathering to announce the launch of FivestarMan. I asked George Sawyer to speak at the event. I had known George Sawyer for eighteen years at the time. He is the lead pastor of a great church in Decatur, Alabama, a church known for its passionate pursuit of winning souls. Thousands of people have experienced life change at Calvary Assembly.

After I had shared the concept of FivestarMan with George, he implemented the message and strategy at Calvary. It has worked! Thousands of men have changed their lives and stepped up to be the husbands and fathers God intended them to be. Although it is a simple strategy, the FivestarMan Initiative works. Hundreds of churches are implementing it. George and Calvary Assembly were the first to test it.

When George spoke to that small gathering to launch FivestarMan, he spoke the message that you are about to read. When I heard it, I realized that God had given him a clarion call—a challenging message that every man needs to hear. The *Resurrection of Authentic Manhood* is a clear and distinguished call to men to step out of the grave of dead manhood and walk into the lives God originally intended for them to live.

You will read this book with great anticipation. As you go through its pages you will find yourself on the edge of your seat, wanting to stand up. You will want to look at yourself in the mirror and declare in a loud voice, "Get up and be a man!"

—Neil Kennedy

INTRODUCTION

The teen was too young to enlist in the military, but this was war. America had been surprisingly and brutally attacked and he had to do his part. The year was 1941, the original "9-11" and "ground zero" was Honolulu.

With some creative information given concerning his age, he was accepted, and he enlisted in the navy. In short order he would be aboard a destroyer escort and engaged in a raging war in the South Pacific. Death was ever present as island by island was recaptured from the enemy. Hostile warplanes attempted to bomb, strafe, or actually crash into his ship kamikaze-style.

He survived this dance with death and returned home to a relieved and thankful family who had unceasingly prayed for him. Like many returning veterans from World War II, he did his best to resume his life. He married, began a family, and started a career, but something was missing.

What was this void deep within his heart?

Life was full and promising. Death had been left far behind in the South Pacific, and yet it seemed that a place within him was entombed.

Then his world changed. From a source he had doubted and even ignored, the answer came. The God who had protected him in war now became the God who saved him in life.

Jesus Christ stepped through the door the man opened, and finally the man was totally alive. He had been resurrected! His resurrection to new life in Christ not only transformed his life, it affected us all.

This man was my father.

I grew up with the incredible honor of living with an authentic man as my hero. The legacy of his godly life is incalculable and continues on to this day through the successive generations of his loving, grateful family.

This book is your invitation to join the revolution of resurrected manhood. It is the clarion call to all men who are still searching to understand what is missing, the dead places, and the voids that they have in their lives.

Even now, I hear the footsteps of your Savior as He walks toward the door of your heart.

Your resurrection is waiting.

CHAPTER ONE
LAZARUS IS DEAD

It all seemed so final—so hopeless. The body of a man who had died before his time had been laid in a cold, stone tomb, and a huge rock had been pushed across the entrance. Death had taken a captive.

Outside the tomb the grieving family slowly walked away, clutching each other and wiping their tears, trying to understand how this could have happened and how they would now live with this void in their lives. The one they loved and needed was gone. Their lives would forever be changed. Who would replace him? Who would hold them together? Grief and fear of the future hung heavy like a black mourner's robe draped on their shoulders.

Inside the tomb, nothing stirred. There was no breathing, no rhythmic beating of the heart, no life. The body slowly grew as cold as the stone slab upon which it had been laid. There was no movement, no sound, no laughter. There was only the stark and stunning contrast of the strong and vital man, who only a few hours before had been the source of so much life and promise.

The hours slowly went by. Life continued, but how different it had become. One day merged into another and then another and another. It seemed that the man's death had entombed them all.

Then, unbelievably and unexpectedly, it happened! It began inside that dark, cold prison of a tomb, in the very center of death, the stronghold of lost hope. Life erupted!

> The rumble of the resurrection of authentic manhood has begun!

His eyes fluttered. His breath returned. His heart was beating, and that infectious smile was back on his face again. And the laughter of pure joy, of total victory, reverberated off the walls of that rocky sepulcher as the huge stone rolled away and Resurrection Life conquered death!

Jesus Christ had triumphed over death and opened the door of hope and life for all mankind. Salvation, freedom, and resurrection of lost hopes and dreams, is God's gift to everyone. But it is received individually, one person at a time.

Lazarus experienced his resurrection moment. Now, sir, it is your turn!

In fact, it is our turn. The victory of Jesus Christ and what we learn from the resurrection of Lazarus will launch a movement. The rumble of the resurrection of authentic manhood has begun!

Right where you are, it has begun. You may be at your lowest moment. You may be farther away from God than you have ever been in your life. You may feel that all your dreams are dead and your purpose has been imprisoned.

But God can reach you even at this place in your life. It is not too late!

As you take this journey with Lazarus through these pages, you will discover the man God created you to be. This is your open door. There is more to you than the shallow, selfish caricature of present-day manhood! There is a deep desire inside you to be a man of character and strength, a man who is respected and loved by those closest to you. You can be released from the weakest and worst lifestyle and resurrected to life at the highest level through Christ. This is in your DNA. God designed you to be an authentic man. When you connect your life with His, He enables you to become the great and noble man who is waiting to be released from deep within your heart.

Everything has a genesis. Everything has a beginning. Every earthquake has an epicenter. Every hurricane has an eye. Every movement has a place where it begins. It's incredible that you and I are at the ground zero of this movement. Today we can be the epicenter of this resurrection earthquake that rattles and awakens manhood around the world.

This is what I know: To bring about something new in your life, there has to be a turning point. There has to be a time when you decide, "God, things are going to be different for me. I'm going to believe bigger than I have believed. I'm going to see what I haven't seen. Lord, I'm going to let You shape me. I'm going to let You determine the kind of man I'm going to become."

Why this desperate call for resurrection?

Studies nationwide have shown that children growing up in homes where a father is not present are much more likely to live in poverty and be at higher risk for illegal drug and alcohol use. Girls without the consistent influence of a loving father are more susceptible to the pressure to get involved in pre-marital sex at younger ages and, consequently, many become pregnant as teens. And the emotional stress of single mothers trying to raise their children without the support and love of a good male role model in the home frequently leads to higher levels of emotional insecurity of their children, which directly affects their educational and vocational success later in life.

> God is not willing to simply stand by and mourn the death of genuine manhood.

The staggering effects of authentic manhood's death are everywhere. It is far too late to consider incremental evolutionary changes. The urgent cries of the women and children of our culture mandate a sweeping revolutionary resurrection!

Something has happened to authentic manhood. There has been a diminishing and a departure from God's original design and intent. As our culture has drifted farther away from God and replaced His design with substitutes and counterfeits, we have lost our way. Society has incrementally beaten down and weakened authentic manhood. Weakness leads to sickness, and untreated sickness ultimately leads to death.

But God is not willing to simply stand by and mourn the death of genuine manhood. God is going to resurrect it in you.

If you will let Him.

Lazarus grew sick and finally died, but he was resurrected. He was given another chance. He found new life, and so can you.

Let's follow his story.

> *Now a man named Lazarus was sick. He was from*
> *Bethany, the village of Mary and her sister Martha.*
> *(This Mary, whose brother Lazarus now lay sick,*
> *was the same one who poured perfume on the Lord*
> *and wiped his feet with her hair.) So the sisters sent*
> *word to Jesus, "Lord, the one you love is sick."*
>
> *John 11:1–3*

In the gospel of John, we are given the opportunity to view the events surrounding the sickness, death, and resurrection of Lazarus, the friend of Jesus. Incredible insights are revealed as we understand that there are prophetic aspects between the biblical account of the death of Lazarus and the death of manhood in society today. As we study this story, we see startling parallels to the attitudes and actions transpiring in the culture today that are indicative of the emasculation of the men of our nation.

The news came to Jesus, "The one you love is sick."

The struggles in your life matter to God. He loves you even when you have stopped loving yourself. The desperate condition of manhood today has not escaped the attention of God. He is ready and willing to step into your life just as He did for Lazarus.

Jesus told the religious leaders of His day why He was willing to get close to men struggling with sin. "It is not the healthy who need a doctor, but the sick. . . . I desire mercy, not sacrifice. For I have not come to call the righteous, but sinners" (Matthew 9:12–13). That's good news for men who will be honest with themselves, who realize what is broken in their lives can only be restored by God.

When Jesus arrived on the scene in Bethany, Lazarus had died. Lazarus was not merely sleeping. Medicine could not rouse him. The cries of the mourners proclaimed loud and clear that death had conquered life. Mortality had claimed another victim. Mary and Martha were devastated.

"He's dead. It's too late. Nothing can be done. No one can help him, not even Jesus"—or so they thought.

This mindset has permeated our society today. Instead of contending for healthy, God-designed manhood, it seems we have rolled over and accepted the confused and weakened substitutes that are paraded before us in a constant media barrage. We are told that Jesus is either irrelevant or incapable of healing the wounds of our lives, and so our concept of authentic manhood is left to weaken and die.

No one thought Jesus could help Lazarus once he had died. But Jesus did!

Many think that it's too late for Jesus to resurrect manhood today. But He will! He came to Lazarus and He has come to us. Don't give up. Don't give in.

Recently it was my privilege to hear a young father and husband tell his "back from death" testimony.

He and his wife were standing before the judge in divorce court. In the eyes of man it was over. Their marriage had died. But before the final divorce decree, the judge asked them to search their hearts to see if, perhaps, they might still love each other. Then the judge firmly stated that he would not grant them a divorce that day. They would have to return to court at a later date.

The couple never went back. God resurrected a man, and with him, a wife, two children, their marriage, their home, and their lives. Ten years later they are loving God and growing together in Him as a happy family.

No matter what anyone says, it's not over until the One who conquered death triumphs in victory!

Without question, manhood is under attack in our generation. Masculinity is on its deathbed. It is not simply resting. Self-help strategies will not revive it. Culture has claimed genuine manhood as its victim. Society parades by the casket and our women and children are left desolate.

CHAPTER TWO
THE ORIGINAL DESIGN OF MAN

Is this what God intended? Is this all we can expect out of life?

Absolutely not!

Before we can understand what is to be resurrected, we must first look at what has died. If something needs to be resurrected, it means it was once alive and vital but, for some reason, it has died. To resurrect manhood in the world, we first have to take a look at the original plan and purpose of God to see what man was meant to be.

We find the original purposes for man at the very outset of the Bible in the first chapter of the book of Genesis.

What did God do in the beginning? What was the plan of God for man? What did man look like when God created him?

We've lost the picture of what a man was intended to be in God's creation.

> Man was designed by God to fulfill a purpose and walk in a unique identity.

Deep inside every man is a voice straining to roar with authentic manhood. Inside every man, God has placed the heart of a champion. There is a warrior inside you. God's intent is for you to reach dreams that are greater than you have ever imagined, because, as large as your own dreams may be, God is able to do exceedingly, abundantly above all you could ever ask or imagine, according to His power at work inside you (Ephesians 3:20). You are a roaring lion, poised to take your place as a godly man in this world.

Your voice may be quiet at this moment. You may have given up on your dreams. You may have pushed your masculinity down and buried it under layers of disappointment, failure, guilt, or shame.

That's not God's design. He is the Resurrection and the Life.

This book—this declaration—is not just a slap on the wrist or a rebuke to shape up. God has real answers. In Him we find powerful hope, healing, and total restoration of everything that the enemy has stolen from the men of this generation.

How did we get offtrack and how can we be raised to new life?

We must look to God's Word to find real understanding, real help, and real change.

> *Then God said, "Let us make man in our image, in our likeness, and let them rule over the fish of the sea and the birds of the air, over the livestock, over*

*all the earth, and over all the creatures that move
along the ground." So God created man in his own
image, in the image of God he created him; male
and female he created them. God blessed them and
said to them, "Be fruitful and increase in number;
fill the earth and subdue it. Rule over the fish of the
sea and the birds of the air and over every living
creature that moves on the ground."*

Genesis 1:26–28

The first thing God did was to create the earth and fashion it.
Then God the Father, the Son, and the Holy Spirit—the triune
God—said, *"Let us make man in our image, in our likeness."*

What an incredible beginning! God created man. Man was
designed by God to fulfill a purpose and walk in a unique identity.

When God created man, He didn't look at the animals. He didn't
look at the plants. He didn't choose any other pattern for the
creation of man but Himself. He didn't speak to the ground, to
the sky or to the water. He looked within Himself and said, "It's
time for Me to create the crowning glory of all creation. It's time
for Me to bring forth something that will represent Me for eons
of time. It's time for Me to bring forth someone who will stand in
My authority and fulfill the image of a servant leader to remind
the inhabitants of earth that there is a God in heaven, so I'm
going to create man."

This is what God designed every man to be. You are formed from
the pattern of God's image and likeness. That was His original
plan. God made man to be His representative on this earth. He
created this planet with you in mind. You're a steward of all His
creation. He created you. He positioned you. He trusts you. When
you learn to walk with Him, you'll discover who you really are.

You're intelligent. You're strong spiritually, mentally, and physically.

These are the qualities God originally designed you to have. It's time they are resurrected and come to the forefront in your life.

Understand that this is not talking about what you *ought to be.* This is *who you are.* It's not talking about what you *need to learn.* It's talking about what you *need to release.* All these things are already inside of you. God placed them there, and only God can enable you to walk in them.

> A true biblical blessing imparts something supernatural to the one who receives it.

God said, "I'm going to create man in *My image* and in *My likeness.*"

Notice the very first thing God did as He looked within Himself to create mankind. He created and designed them male and female, and then God blessed them.

The word *blessing*, when used in Scripture, doesn't just mean uttering a short little prayer under your breath when someone sneezes. A true biblical blessing imparts something supernatural to the one who receives it. It's not something a man can get by himself. It's something that only comes from God.

When God created Adam in His image and likeness, He told Adam, "Before you begin your journey of destiny, I'm going to bless you. I'm going to speak an impartation of my power that will empower you and cause you to be endued with the ability to fulfill the purpose for which I created you."

He blessed Adam and Eve and told them to be fruitful, to

increase in number (to multiply), to fill the earth, to subdue it, and to have dominion. They were to rule over the fish of the sea, the birds of the air, and over every living creature that moved on the ground. In short, your God-designed DNA gives you the ability to bring about increase and to use every resource God created for you to succeed as a godly overcomer in this life.

God made man and woman, and it was good. As a man, you are able to perfectly connect to a woman and be a godly husband and a godly father. You have that capacity. This is not about your grandfather or your family tree. You may have been born into a very ungodly, dysfunctional family. The pattern of your family may be one of infidelity, abuse, adultery, and divorce. You may have been born that way, but you have not been "born again" that way.

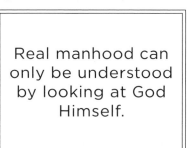

Real manhood can only be understood by looking at God Himself.

When you submit your life to Christ and trust Him to become your Savior, the power of sin is broken off of your life and God's original plan for you is resurrected.

God designed you to be a one-woman man, to have a godly home, to connect with your family, and to become everything you've dreamed a husband and father could be. This is not who you *have to be*—it's who you *want to be*. This is the man who comes alive when the resurrection power of Jesus Christ enters your life!

God created man in His own image and likeness. Man was not fallen. He was not lacking. He was not missing any power or ability. Man was created to be like God in character and nature. Real manhood can only be understood by looking at God Himself.

The Creator of the universe has given you authority and ability. According to His original plan and intent, you were designed to walk with Him as an authentic man.

A real man does not lead by intimidation or fear but by the power of his character and the inspiration of his identity. He is a man who leads by serving his Creator. He is a true servant leader. He is a man who is secure in himself, who doesn't derive his sense of self-esteem from his accomplishments or his exploits with women. He knows his identity comes from almighty God. He understands that he is strongest when he is on his knees in the presence of God. He is truly powerful when the Word of God is dwelling richly within him. This is the man God created you to be. You are His representative on this planet.

> As you walk in relationship with Him, you have been given rulership under Him.

Don't say you can't read your Bible. Don't say you don't know how to pray. Don't say you can't hear from God.

You were created to walk in the very presence of God Almighty. You have the capacity to know His voice. You were created to be His companion, to walk with Him, and to represent Him on this earth. You're His friend. His Spirit lives inside of you.

As you walk in relationship with Him, you have been given rulership under Him. When you live as God created you to live, life works. When you learn to connect with Him, you learn how to go forward and walk in your God-given authority.

My good friend Neil Kennedy sums up God's original intent for man in his book, *FIVESTARMAN: The Five Passions of Authentic Manhood*. Neil makes it clear that to understand and exhibit the characteristics of authentic manhood, we must realize that God has placed five unique qualities and purposes of a godly man within us. Proverbs 20:5 declares: *"The purposes of a man's heart are deep waters, but a man of understanding draws them out."* As we walk in God's original intent for our lives, we release and draw out these five godly purposes and become the authentic men—the FivestarMen—God has called us to become.

A FIVESTARMAN IS:

ADVENTUROUS

You have a God-given passion for adventure. True men seek out new challenges with determination. Women relate to each other face-to-face, drinking tea. Men relate to each other shoulder-to-shoulder, facing a task together. When little boys meet in school, the first thing they want to do is compete. Who is the fastest? Who is the strongest? Who can hit the ball farther than anyone else? As a man, you need a challenge. You are at your best when you are reaching, stretching your limits, taking on new opportunities. Your eyes scan the far horizons. You wonder what challenges await you. Do you have what it takes? Your eyes have sight, but it's your heart that has vision. Deep in your heart, you hear the voice of God saying, "Join with me and begin this great adventure." You must find a band of authentic men and join together with them to do great things for God.

ENTREPRENEURIAL

You're passionate about new ideas and sources to create income so you can provide for your family and do the things that are right. You are not only capable of holding a job, but you also have the God-given ability to create income from new channels. You not only serve God on Sunday in a church building, but you also have discovered that you can use your unique, God-given gifts and talents in the marketplace. Your pastor and your church will provide you vision to succeed and serve God in every phase of life, and in return your increase will produce provision for the vision of your church.

GALLANT

You are a defender of women and children. You live a life of honor and respect. The weak and less fortunate are safe around you because you're a godly man. It's time that gallantry is resurrected and brought back into our culture. Our society is desperately searching for men of this quality. Children are always safe and protected in your presence. Women are secure, honored, and always treated as ladies. You treat younger women as if they were your daughters. Women of your own age are treated as if they were your sisters. An older woman is respected as if she were your mother. And, as a married man, your wife holds a place of such honor in your life that she alone has your eyes and your passion.

FAITHFUL

You're a faithful man, unwavering in what you believe. God will never expect from you what He has not equipped you to be. You have the capacity to be faithful to your God, to your family, and to the things that you know are true. The authentic man realizes that true freedom can only be discovered when he trusts his life to God. Your strength is not only found in the might of your muscles, but it is also forged in the fire of your determination to keep your word and honor your promises. You can be counted on. You are a man of principle. You may never be famous or well known. Public accolades and medals may not come your way. But those who know you best will know the blessing of living under the shelter of a faithful man. Your Heavenly Father rejoices over a son who has proven to be trustworthy in all his ways.

PHILANTHROPIC

Deep inside you want to live a life that is bigger than yourself. Living only for your own interests can never satisfy you. You want to leave a legacy. You want to devote your resources and actions to champion and connect with a worthy cause. In a recent national poll Americans were asked to state their greatest fear. With all the rare diseases, threats of terrorism, and reports of natural disasters that scream at us from our news sources, the results of this poll were quite a surprise. The number-one greatest fear of the American public was that they would have lived their lives and never have made a positive difference in their world. When you surrender and connect your life with God, you become a unique and integral part of the greatest message and movement of hope on the planet today. To make a lasting impact, to make a difference, you must leave behind more than you take in life. You are generous and giving with your time and resources. You realize that you make a living by what you get, but you make a life by what you give. When you hold a seed tightly in your hand, that is all it will ever be, but when you share that seed in the name of Christ, its potential is unlimited. Philanthropic men live to give.

Now we can understand this verse more clearly.

> *The purposes of a man's heart are deep waters, but*
> *a man of understanding draws them out.*
>
> *Proverbs 20:5*

When men begin to walk with God in line with His original intent, they begin to grow and be strengthened. But if we depart from the image God placed within us, counterfeits and substitutes will creep into our lives.

Unfortunately society has told us that, as men, we must break away and establish our own freedom. This is a lie from the very heart of Satan, the one who has come to steal, kill, and destroy our manhood. As we have pursued the unattainable goal of complete independence and personal freedom, true masculinity has been buried under sin, rebellion, dysfunction, and confusion.

How do we then respond to this attack on authentic manhood?

The answer is clear. We counter it with a firsthand revelation of the Savior's power through a personal relationship with Jesus Christ.

Almighty God releases His power in us as we commit our lives to Him. Christianity isn't an event; it's a relationship. It's not a sprint; it's a lifelong journey. As we walk that journey, we will begin to live the lives God designed us to live.

Let's not settle for anything less.

CHAPTER THREE
SEPARATION SICKNESS

We've seen a clear and compelling picture of God's original plan for man, but now we stand in need of a resurrection to recapture this image in our lives. The image of godly manhood has suffered and died in most arenas of our current culture. Manhood today is not what God intended it to be. But there are isolated pockets of encouragement and hope. There are men who are standing up today and leading. This is a sign of the end times. Men in the church are waking up and hearing the call of God, but, as a whole, the men of society are in a red-alert crisis.

We don't need *evolution*. We need a *revolution*. We don't need something that is slowly going to creep through. We need a holy shock straight to the heart of a system that is dead. We need a resurrection that can only come from almighty God.

I'm reminded of one of the most traumatic moments of my life.

My father had just suffered a massive heart attack. As we rushed to the emergency room of the hospital, we were met by the emergency room nurse and informed that my father had a very slim chance of survival. As his heart failed again, the doctor called for the defibrillator as a last resort. My father was dying. There was no time for casual talk or half-hearted attempts to save him. His shirt was ripped open. The highly charged paddles were placed on his chest, and everyone was instructed to stand clear, all hands off. The electricity surged through his body. It was a risky decision with the condition of my father's heart at that moment, but it saved his life.

> Only the power of the same Spirit that raised Christ from the dead will save manhood in this hour.

It's time the church boldly declares to all the pretenders and contenders, "All hands off! Stand back. This is God's moment!" Only the power of the same Spirit that raised Christ from the dead will save manhood in this hour.

Lazarus was sick. He was weakened by some infirmity. Lazarus was not at his full strength or capacity. That's a picture of manhood today. Masculinity has been weakened. Man, created in the image and likeness of God, is barely a shadow of what he used to be.

How did this happen? How did God's original plan waste away to nothing?

What happened to authentic manhood?

As we listen through the scriptures to the voices of those closest to Lazarus, we begin to see a picture and receive a revelation of what weakened, incapacitated, and ultimately buried true manhood today.

"Lord," Martha said to Jesus, "if you had been here, my brother would not have died."

John 11:21

When Mary reached the place where Jesus was and saw him, she fell at his feet and said, "Lord, if you had been here, my brother would not have died."

John 11:32

First Martha, then Mary, expressed to Jesus. "If only you had been here, my brother would not have died." That statement is the key to the death of authentic manhood.

Lazarus died when Jesus was not with him. Genuine manhood died when man began walking away from the presence of God.

The infirmity that has choked the life out of masculinity in this generation is separation sickness.

If we were walking connected to God as the source of our lives, we would not be incrementally wasting away, dying by degrees.

We are constantly inundated with distorted depictions of manhood today. In the absence of a genuine relationship with Christ, counterfeit images have arisen and lowered the bar. This is not the time to rewrite the rules in the middle of the game. Our greatest need in this hour is not to find someone to tell us it's okay to give up and give in or sit by while potentially great men, great fathers, and husbands are euthanized on the altars of confused compromise. What we do need—what we must have—is a fresh, clear, compelling encounter with the living God who is the author and source of what an authentic man is supposed to be. If we were really drawing upon His strength and power, we wouldn't be weak; we wouldn't be infirm. Manhood would not be in its tomb.

When God creates something, He defines its future and assigns its destiny. For it to thrive, it must remain connected to the source from which God created it.

> *Then God said, "Let the land produce vegetation:*
> *seed-bearing plants and trees on the land that bear*
> *fruit with seed in it, according to their various*
> *kinds." And it was so. The land produced vegeta-*
> *tion: plants bearing seed according to their kinds*
> *and trees bearing fruit with seed in it according to*
> *their kinds. And God saw that it was good.*
>
> *Genesis 1:11–12*

> *And God said, "Let the water teem with living*
> *creatures, and let birds fly above the earth across*
> *the expanse of the sky." So God created the great*
> *creatures of the sea and every living and moving*
> *thing with which the water teems, according to*
> *their kinds, and every winged bird according to its*
> *kind. And God saw that it was good.*
>
> *Genesis 1:20–21*

> *And God said, "Let the land produce living crea-*
> *tures according to their kinds: livestock, creatures*
> *that move along the ground, and wild animals,*
> *each according to its kind." And it was so.*
>
> *Genesis 1:24*

When God was ready to create vegetation, He spoke to the ground. He told the land to produce vegetation, and the plants were there. When God was ready to create fish and creatures of the sea, He spoke to the water, and the fish and aquatic creatures appeared in the ocean. When God was ready to create livestock and wild animals, He spoke to the earth and the animals appeared according to His design.

The plants and livestock sprang forth from the soil. The fish sprang forth from the water. When God creates something, He always connects it to its source. When God creates something, the source from which He draws it determines that creation's strength and potential.

> The strength and vitality of man is determined by staying connected to his source.

> *Then God said, "Let us make man in our image, in our likeness . . ."*

> *Genesis 1:26*

When God was ready to create man, He did not speak to the ground. He did not speak to the water. He did not speak to the clouds. When God created man, *He spoke to Himself.*

You were created, brought forth, designed, and assigned to live your life from the very essence of God.

The strength and vitality of man is determined by staying connected to his source. If you take a plant out of the earth, it withers and dies within a few days. If you take a fish out of water, it suffocates in a few short minutes. If you drop a lion in the middle of the sea—no matter how strong it is—the majestic beast will drown in a matter of hours. A lion was created to be a powerful force only when he is in his element—on dry ground.

If a man separates himself from the presence of God, he will die. He may be physically existing, emotionally functioning, and mentally moving along, but if he is disconnected from the presence of God, he becomes dead in his trespasses and sins. He has robbed himself of his identity. He has separated himself from the source of his life and denied himself his potential.

You see, I can determine your potential if I can identify your source. You were created out of God Himself. He birthed you out of who He is and said, "Let this man be."

Why did Lazarus die?

"Lord, if only You had been here."

If you stay connected to your Source, you won't suffer from the decaying sickness of separation. You won't lose the vitality of true masculinity. Separation from God creates a void, and because nature abhors a vacuum, that void must be filled. Separation sickness has caused the men of our day to try to fill their emptiness with everything but the genuine presence of God.

My heart breaks for the men of this generation, and so does the heart of God. So few have had the privilege of growing up in the presence of a genuine godly father or male role model. There has been no one to follow, no one to emulate. Men have been left to themselves.

But if you listen, you can hear the sound of the footsteps of God outside the tomb—outside of your tomb. Resurrection help has arrived!

From the dawn of human history God came to walk with man in the cool of the day. When Adam sinned it wasn't God running from man; it was man running from God. God is not avoiding you. He is not hiding. He is searching for you, calling for you even now.

When Adam separated himself, he came to a terrible realization. "I'm uncovered. I'm naked and exposed. I'm not the man I thought I was." Instead of running back to God to connect himself to God's original design and life, Adam turned to a substitute. He grabbed a leaf from a tree in the garden and covered himself. The moment Adam plucked the leaf from its branch, it began dying in his hand.

> My heart breaks for the men of this generation, and so does the heart of God.

Everything I turn to as a substitute for the presence of God in my life begins to wither the moment it touches my hand.

Unfortunately, today's men are barely a shadow of what they could be. With so few authentic godly men present as role models, they are left to reach for one substitute after another. They grow weaker and weaker, separated from God.

Over the centuries man has disengaged himself from God. Man has created counterfeits for true worship. In our "devolved" society, we may not worship idols made out of wood and stone. We're sophisticated enough not to sacrifice our children to pagan deities, but an idol is anything man creates with his own ability and puts between himself and almighty God. There are scores of idols being worshipped by men in our society. Some of these idols have been set up in churches. Some have been set up in our economy. Some have been set up in our businesses. They have become a part of our entertainment and recreation. In virtually every area that a man finds himself engaged today, idols have come between man and His Creator.

You must never forget: The Devil works in gaps but God works in connections.

The Devil incessantly works to create separation between you and God. It is in these gaps that he will wedge himself and his strategies of destruction to constantly leverage you away from God and His purposes for your life. Those small gaps of willful choices become open doors to much greater consequences. Someone once stated that sin will take you farther than you planned on going; it will keep you longer than you planned on staying and cost you much more than you planned on paying.

Satan works in gaps.

> *When an evil spirit comes out of a person, it goes through arid places seeking rest and does not find it. Then it says, 'I will return to the house I left.' When it arrives, it finds the house swept clean and put in order. Then it goes and takes seven other spirits more wicked than itself, and they go in and live there. And the final condition of that man is worse than the first.*
>
> *Luke 11:24–26*

Gaps are dangerous. The enemy seeks to fill them with an ever-increasing separation sickness. The only way to cure the void of a gap is to fill it with something more powerful. When a gap is filled with the life of God, Satan's influence in that area of your life is broken.

The Bible explains gaps and connections in this way:

> *You, dear children, are from God and have overcome them, because the one who is in you is greater than the one who is in the world.*
>
> *1 John 4:4*

God's Word makes it simple and clear:

> *Do not be overcome with evil, but overcome evil with good.*
>
> *Romans 12:21*

If I create a gap instead of a connection with God, something will automatically rush in to try to fill that space. If I dig up a tree in my yard and do not fill in the hole left behind, nature decides what will fill that void. When it rains the hole is filled with water. If it snows the hole is filled with snow. The only control

> Apart from Him, you can do nothing. Connected to Him, nothing is impossible for you to do.

I have concerning this hole is for me to choose what will fill it and when it will be filled, and then I must fill in the void. It will still continue to rain and snow but that won't matter any more because the gap has been closed.

It's a natural law that the void left by any gap must be filled.

If I am naked physically, my natural instinct will take over to try to cover myself. If I am naked spiritually, I may try to cover myself with dead religion. But it's dying the moment I put my hand on it. I may try to cover myself by living behind a façade, acting as if I've got it all together and everything is fine. But eventually decay will set in and choke the life out of me.

Genuine manhood has withered because of separation from God. We have removed ourselves from our source. We've tried to live as though everything is okay, but we're fish out of water. We're plants ripped from the ground. Death is imminent.

> *I am the vine; you are the branches. If a man*
> *remains in me and I in him, he will bear much fruit;*
> *apart from me you can do nothing.*

> *John 15:5*

Today we have the opportunity to say, "God, I want to reconnect. I'm tired of the substitutes and lies. I'm tired of living my life as if everything is okay when it's not."

It's that simple.

Apart from Him, you can do nothing. Connected to Him, nothing is impossible for you to do.

You must stay connected to God and His original plan for your life. You need a download of the Holy Spirit every day you live. You need to learn to walk in the truth of the Word of God. It's not required for you to pray in King James English. You do not need a theology degree to stay connected to your God. You don't need to know all the nuances of this or that doctrine, how many angels can stand on the head of a pin or what day Jesus is coming back. All you need to know is that if you stay connected to your source and abide in Him, nothing will be impossible in your life.

CHAPTER FOUR
THE VOID OF DEATH

W hat has happened to authentic manhood?

What happens if you don't address sickness in your body?

We're all familiar with the old adage, "Time heals all wounds." But that axiom is not true if you have cancer. Given enough time and left untreated, even the smallest spot of cancer will eventually kill you. If you allow disease to go unchecked in your body, it will kill you.

Though the Bible doesn't say what type of malady Lazarus was suffering from, whatever it was, Lazarus was apparently sick for quite some time and he eventually died.

> *On his arrival, Jesus found that Lazarus had*
> *already been in the tomb for four days. Now Beth-*

any was less than two miles from Jerusalem, and many Jews had come to Martha and Mary to comfort them in the loss of their brother.

John 11:17–19

> When authentic manhood dies, the whole structure begins to shift to fill man's role.

When Jesus arrived on the scene, Lazarus was dead. He had already been in the tomb four days. Jesus found Mary and Martha crying. He found the whole neighborhood crying in the void that surrounded the death of Lazarus.

In America today we find society crying in the wake of the death of manhood. We find little children crying. We find abandoned women crying. We find millions of people weeping at the tomb of masculinity. Broken hearts. Broken dreams. Destroyed hopes. They're weeping at the tomb of manhood that is dead in our culture. They are not really sure why their lives are so hard; they only know something is missing. Something is out of order. Their loss is profound.

> *When Jesus saw her weeping, and the Jews who had come along with her also weeping, he was deeply moved in spirit and troubled.*
>
> *John 11:33*

When authentic manhood dies, a void is created. People weep. Relationships begin to shift.

In our culture today, relationships have shifted to fill the void. When authentic manhood dies, the whole structure begins to shift to fill man's role. He's gone. He's absent. And the people left behind are scrambling to fill the void left in his wake.

Single moms are wearily trying to work their jobs and the jobs of absentee fathers. Relationships have shifted in the absence of genuine manhood and, as a result, children are raising children because their mothers must now become both mom and dad in their homes.

Relationships are out of order. Families are dysfunctional. Before we get upset at "women's rights" movements, we might need to think about what women are trying to do to survive in the absence of true men. Before we get dismayed about the decaying state of traditional families today, maybe we need to realize that all of our dysfunction—all of this relational shifting—is the result of men not being present in the home.

Absentee fatherhood is epidemic in our culture today. It is a deadly disease, which if left untreated, will cause even more death and destruction in our society.

You may not realize it, but absentee fatherhood comes in two different forms. Some fathers simply desert their families and walk away, while others deny their families their love and guidance. Some absentee fathers simply choose to leave their homes and children behind and don't provide for them. They're what society calls "deadbeat dads." (This is an almost prophetic title alluding to the roots of death found in their counterfeit identities.)

What these men have chosen to do is wrong, but I wonder if they have ever seen what is right? Did their fathers leave them?

Of course, this is no excuse, but there has to be a solution. A generation is literally dying to be fathered. A movement of resurrected, restored men of God is the only solution for our broken, weeping families. It's not too late for you to be used to break this deadly repeating cycle.

The second type of "deadbeat dads" is made up of millions of absentee fathers who faithfully go to their homes after work every night but turn on the television or grab the newspaper and shut themselves off to everyone around them. These disconnected fathers might as well not come home at all for all the good they do for their wives and children. Their kids never hear the words, "I love you," "I receive you," or "I believe in you." These fathers-in-name-only are running here and there, busy with work and hobbies, never showing their children that they are important—never spending any time or thought on their sons and daughters. And in the absence of their fathers (dead men from poverty level all the way up into the elite social groups of society) little boys are growing up not knowing how to please their fathers or seeing how a real man looks, talks, or acts. Little girls craving the attention of a healthy father-daughter relationship become painfully vulnerable to the selfish advances of every male (or female) predator.

> Children are left to decide for themselves who their role models will be, because heroic men have not guided them.

Remember that an authentic man is a gallant man. The spirit of gallantry says, "I'm going to treat older women as if they were my mother. I will treat women in my peer group as my sisters. I will treat young girls as I would treat my own daughters." Children are safe around a real man. His protective arm covers them. Yet when we look into our society, we find that our children are being abused by all kinds of authority figures.

How could this have happened to our world?

It has happened because children are desperately looking for someone to walk into their lives and fill the void left by the death of authentic manhood. They've been exposed to evil because they're not covered. Children are left to decide for themselves who their role models will be, because heroic men have not guided them. In the void, some of the most outlandish "heroes" have rushed in to deceive them and make them feel recognized, accepted, and loved.

While we appreciate all that the ladies have done and their determination to follow God with or without the men, we need to have a new identity in the church if we're going to accomplish the destiny that God has called us to fulfill.

God is raising up a new breed of man. We're going to experience a resurrection. Man is on his deathbed, but there is Someone on the way to raise him up.

There are incredibly deep-seated needs spiraling through our culture today because manhood is dying. As much as we may like to believe that all is well, all is not well. Our relationships just continue to mutate. We're not evolving; we're "devolving," desperately trying to find a way to fulfill the vacant roles left by the cessation of authentic manhood.

Disorder brings dysfunction. Dysfunction creates abuse.

That's where we are today.

CHAPTER FIVE
THE MOURNERS

We've seen the response of the family to the death of authentic manhood, but look with me at another group we never hear about until this moment. We find that not only was Mary weeping, but the mourners were also weeping. Upon closer examination these mourners carried a different sound. Their lack of genuine grief released a sickening aroma like the smell of a cheap perfume.

> *When Mary heard this, she got up quickly and went to him. Now Jesus had not yet entered the village, but was still at the place where Martha had met him. When the Jews who had been with Mary in the house, comforting her, noticed how quickly she got up and went out, they followed her, supposing she was going to the tomb to mourn there. When Mary reached the place where Jesus was and saw him,*

*she fell at his feet and said, "Lord, if you had been
here, my brother would not have died." When Jesus
saw her weeping, and the Jews who had come
along with her also weeping, he was deeply moved
in spirit and troubled.*

John 11:29–33

When Mary reached the place where Jesus was and she saw Him,
she fell at His feet. When Jesus saw Mary and the Jews who had
come along with her weeping, He was deeply moved in spirit and
troubled. By the time Jesus arrived on the scene, the mourners
had taken over. They were loudly weeping and wailing. To the
discerning ear their noise was more of a distraction, but those
caught up in the throes of grief were in too much distress to realize the difference. When Mary and Martha got up, the mourners
followed them.

In the Jewish culture, a mourner was a person who was paid to
come and wail, mourn, and cry to put on a show at a funeral.
The thought was the more mourners who were present, the more
important and more loved the deceased person was. Simply
stated, a mourner in that day was someone who made a living off
of death.

We don't have traditions like this at funerals today, yet we have
"mourners" all around us. They are everywhere. Back then
mourners sat around and waited for somebody to pass away.
Then they came crawling from the shadows to profit from the
loss, confusion, and pain of those surviving in the aftermath
of death. A mourner made a handsome profit. In the story of
Lazarus, when Jesus arrived, the mourners were already there.
They were happy the man was gone. If Lazarus hadn't died, the
profiteers would have been unemployed for those four days.

If the death of Lazarus is a picture of the death of authentic manhood, then who are the mourners today?

Who is making a living off of the death of manhood in our culture?

The "mourners" in our society are the counterfeits. They're substitutes. They're the proud, self-centered false images of what real men are supposed to be. They have alternative lifestyles and are the redefiners of the family. They eagerly await the time when the real men of God are dead and gone.

> Just because someone shouts the loudest does not mean that his words carry truth.

These modern-day profiteers, like their predecessors, are sneaking out of the shadows from the dark corners and dredges of society who, in the presence of genuine masculinity, never had a voice. But in the void of real manhood, they begin to rise and make their commotion to turn a buck.

Just because someone shouts the loudest does not mean that his words carry truth. Usually it's just the opposite: the greater the bluster the smaller the man.

Let's look at another story where Jesus had an encounter with mourners in the Scriptures.

> *While Jesus was still speaking, some people came from the house of Jairus, the synagogue leader. "Your daughter is dead," they said. "Why bother the teacher anymore?" Overhearing what they said, Jesus told him, "Don't be afraid; just believe." He did not let anyone follow him except Peter, James and John the brother of James. When*

they came to the home of the synagogue leader,
Jesus saw a commotion, with people crying and
wailing loudly. He went in and said to them, "Why
all this commotion and wailing? The child is not
dead but asleep." But they laughed at him. After
he put them all out, he took the child's father and
mother and the disciples who were with him, and
went in where the child was. He took her by the
hand and said to her, "Talitha koum!" (which
means "Little girl, I say to you, get up!"). Imme-
diately the girl stood up and began to walk around
(she was twelve years old). At this they were com-
pletely astonished.

Mark 5:35–42, NIV 2011

In this passage, Jesus had been rushed to the home of Jairus, the synagogue ruler who had a sick daughter. By the time He arrived, the little girl had died. Knowing who He was and what He could do, Jesus confidently walked into the room where the girl was lying dead and proclaimed, "She's not dead. She's only sleeping."

The mourners laughed Him to scorn.

Just as they did in Bethany, the mourners created a lot of noise when something died. But there is no need for mourners, these people who make their living off of the dead, when life is present. Mourners only have a place where death is king.

These disingenuous voices are making their noise, coming out of the shadows, and profiting off the death of what is right and righteous and godly and strong. The mourners are people who only appear at moments of weakness. They seem to sympathize with your pain, but they really bring their own agenda. They're professionals. They have honed their acting skills to a fine art. They can make you believe that they really care.

But they don't.

Just as they did at the home of Jairus, these greedy posers laugh and mock at the words of Christ and taunt us as we struggle to find our place today.

> If you look around the tomb of dead manhood in America, it is not a pretty sight.

With no where else to turn, the abandoned sons of our society either adopt the mourner's hypocritical concept of the culture, becoming effeminate boys who don't know how to be men, or they become tyrants and felons with no self-control. Along the paths of life, the profiteers are stealing the souls of our young men.

Because manhood has died, boys are gravitating toward becoming effeminate or they are creating their own groups, called gangs, where violence has taken over. These two opposite extremes are desperate attempts to bring some order into the midst of pain, while the purveyors of death are filling their ears with the noise of morality's defeat.

Little girls are growing up without men of God in their lives to show them what real love is. They desperately need someone to protect them and stand up for them. These girls would give anything to have a father's love, protection, security, and safety—but because manhood has died in the world, young women are willing to lose their dignity for any man who will show them any kind of attention.

The wives in our American culture are wearing the ill-fitting pants their husbands have dropped. In their men's de facto absence, these women know that *somebody* has to step in and try to save their families and protect their homes.

Just as it was at the tomb of Lazarus, if you look around the tomb of dead manhood in America, it is not a pretty sight. There are mourners. There are hypocrites. There are those who are making their living off of the death of manhood, and something needs to happen. It looks grim, but there is hope. Just as in the story of Lazarus, with all the death and dysfunction, and all the counterfeits, liars, and mourners, when everyone said all hope was lost, there was a Man—a real man—who walked right into the face of death and conquered it. That same Man will conquer the death of manhood today!

It's important to understand that the problem isn't really the mourners, the counterfeits, or the voices that assail and attack our families and make us feel as if there's no hope. The mourners didn't cause the death of Lazarus. They just capitalized on it.

Well-meaning Christians say all the time, "We're never going to get this thing back. We're never going to change things. There are too many voices from the other direction."

But resurrection has nothing to do with the quantity or the volume of the voices ringing out from the camp of the mourners. All that is necessary to silence them is for Jesus to come on the scene and conquer the grave. As real men begin to rise from the tomb to take their places in this world, the mourners will crawl back into the darkness from which they came.

The solution is not to curse the darkness but to light a candle.

> *Do not be overcome by evil, but overcome evil with good.*
>
> *Romans 12:21*

A godly man, functioning in his position as God designed him to function, will fill the void and turn the day around. The mourners will be forced to shut their mouths and make a hasty retreat. A real man of God will bring a family back in order and set a marriage right.

How can little children who have been hurt and abandoned ever have hope again?

True men of God can give it to them.

In the day of darkness, this can be our finest moment and our greatest hour.

That doesn't mean you have to be perfect, but you must be connected to God. It's not your *perfection*; it's your *direction* that is going get you to your destiny. If you fall down, get up. If you fall down again, get back up. Just keep falling forward.

> A godly man, functioning in his position as God designed him to function, will fill the void and turn the day around.

When real men begin to stand connected to their source, in line with God's original intent, they will fill the vacancy and the movement will be birthed. The incredible movement to resurrect authentic manhood will have the life and power of God pulsating through it.

When Satan and his minions were rejoicing over the death of Jesus Christ, the last thing they ever counted on was that on the third day, the resurrection would be their ultimate defeat.

The enemy may be laughing now, mocking and scorning true masculinity in our generation, but God has a plan to resurrect godly men by the power of His Spirit.

What initially appears to be a setback may just be a set up for one of God's great comebacks. What appeared to be the defeat of Jesus Christ was actually positioning Him for His greatest victory—and ours!

The story of the resurrection presents quite a picture for us: mourning, weeping, crying, death, and voids. No one in the city knew what to do.

But one Man had the proper response to the death of Lazarus. Today He also holds the key to respond to the death of authentic manhood.

CHAPTER SIX
JESUS MEETS THE CHALLENGE

When Mary reached the place where Jesus was and saw him, she fell at his feet and said, "Lord, if you had been here, my brother would not have died." When Jesus saw her weeping, and the Jews who had come along with her also weeping, he was deeply moved in spirit and troubled. "Where have you laid him?" he asked. "Come and see, Lord," they replied. Jesus wept. Then the Jews said, "See how he loved him!" But some of them said, "Could not he who opened the eyes of the blind man have kept this man from dying?" Jesus, once more deeply moved, came to the tomb. It was a cave with a stone laid across the entrance. "Take away the stone," he said.

John 11:32–39

Jesus was deeply moved when He came to the tomb. In the Jewish tradition, the tomb of Lazarus was a cave with a stone across the entrance. We read that as Jesus arrived where Lazarus was buried, Jesus wept. He grieved for Mary and Martha. He loved Lazarus. Unlike the mourners who were paid to put on a show, Jesus was touched with the feeling of their infirmity. He sincerely cared about them. Their pain was His pain. Their sorrow was His sorrow, and He wept.

The account of Jesus weeping in verse 35 and the fact that this is the shortest verse in the Bible has somewhat overshadowed the events of the entire story.

> *When Jesus saw her weeping . . . he was deeply moved in spirit and troubled.*
>
> *John 11:33*

> *Jesus, once more deeply moved, came to the tomb.*
>
> *John 11:38*

As you read verse 35 and picture the raw emotion at the scene, don't misunderstand what Jesus did next. We read about Jesus weeping and, in our English translations of the Bible, we try to wrap our minds around what happened. We read the two verses that say Jesus was "deeply moved," and we tend to think that this means He was still crying. We see those two words and think His compassion was just growing deeper and He wept even harder. We say, "He was *deeply moved.*"

But that's not what this phrase means at all.

When we study the Greek word that is translated as *deeply moved* in verse 33 and in verse 38, we begin to see that there is a common misunderstanding as we try to catch the meaning of the original language. The Greek word *embrimaomai* used in both these verses doesn't mean that Jesus cried. Jesus had stopped crying. It doesn't mean that Jesus was deeply mourning the loss of his friend. He wasn't mourning any more. It doesn't mean that He was troubled and didn't know what was going to happen. He knew exactly what to do.

The literal translation of the word *embrimaomai* means *to snort with anger; to express indignation against something; to threaten harshly; or to rebuke or charge sternly*. The word carries the connotation of a wild stallion snorting with anger to protect his herd when he faces a challenger.

When Jesus was deeply moved, it means that He walked right up to the tomb and said, "Get the stone out of the way!" Then he sternly charged death—the force that had sickened, killed, stolen, and destroyed. He threatened the powers of hell that had taken Lazarus. The picture in the Greek is that Jesus walked up to the tomb and snorted like a powerful horse getting ready to charge into battle. This was so much more than just sympathy or empathy. This would be the death of death!

This is a picture of the Man, Jesus—the perfect combination of authority, power, and compassion. This is not the world's image of Jesus, a frail, reclusive philosopher espousing antiquated stories that have little to do with real men facing real challenges. This is the true identity of the Son of God Almighty, who walked into the face of death and snorted, "Get that stone out of My way!"

He didn't whisper. He didn't ask nicely. He didn't beg or even say, "Please."

Jesus walked up, and in a loud voice commanded, "Death, let go of that man! Lazarus, get up right now!" There was fire within

Jesus—the Man who turned death on its ear.

Suddenly the mourners were unemployed. Suddenly the power of death ran into the shadows. Suddenly everything that had been operating in the enemy's plan had to jump out of the way, because Jesus had confronted the foe that had killed His friend and spoken the word to give manhood one more opportunity.

The response Jesus had to death was different from the response of everyone else that day.

Left to ourselves, we only have sympathy and empathy, but when the Son of God walks into the middle of a death scene, everything changes. When the Source of Creation walks into that which has ceased to exist, there is an innate faith and ability to resurrect that which everyone says is too late and too far gone.

God Almighty can speak one word and everything that death has stolen from man can be regenerated.

Religion tells a man to work his way to God. Earn his way out of his tomb. But how obviously faulty is this kind of thinking?

Dead men are incapacitated. They cannot help themselves. Religion is false hope wrapped in a lie covered in our dying flesh. Jesus did not come to start another dead religion; He came to bring life to the fullest.

What does Jesus do in your impossible moment? Does He stand at a distance and offer meaningless advice or condemn you for your failure?

Not this Savior. Just ask three young Hebrew men who were condemned to die in a hellish furnace because they would not renounce their faith. Their account in Daniel chapter three reveals that when they were thrown into the furnace to die, they were not alone. There was a Fourth Man right there in the furnace with them! God came to them and saved them.

Jesus will do the same for you today. He is the same today as He's always been and He will never change (Hebrews 13:8). He's a real God with real power to save real men.

> God Almighty can speak one word and everything that death has stolen from man can be regenerated.

Jesus terminated Lazarus's death. Jesus said, "Enough is enough."

We need more than sympathy right now. We need to stand up in the power of God and say, "Enough is enough!"

As a man of God, have you had enough in your life? Have you had enough of death's reign in this world?

CHAPTER SEVEN
RESURRECTION!

What we want to do in our society today is just ignore the rotting stench of dying manhood. We want to put a stone over it and ignore it. We want to pretend and go on about our business. But Jesus is not willing for you to live your life less than what He created you to be. He is not willing for our generation—or the generation to come—to live in the void of dying manhood.

> *"Take away the stone," he said. "But, Lord," said Martha, the sister of the dead man, "by this time there is a bad odor, for he has been there four days." Then Jesus said, "Did I not tell you that if you believed, you would see the glory of God?" So they took away the stone. Then Jesus looked up and said, "Father, I thank you that you have heard me. I knew that you always hear me, but I said this for*

the benefit of the people standing here, that they may believe that you sent me." When he had said this, Jesus called in a loud voice, "Lazarus, come out!" The dead man came out, his hands and feet wrapped with strips of linen, and a cloth around his face.

John 11:39–44

In that moment, Lazarus was resurrected. Jesus walked in and confronted death. He didn't let it continue to hold his friend in its grasp.

If we could look into the spirit realm today we would hear that there is a clarion call from the throne of God, charging men everywhere, "Rise up and live again! Stand back up on your feet and be everything God has called you to be."

Even on Easter Sunday morning, the disciples of Jesus still didn't get it. The women were coming to finish embalming the dead body of Jesus. They weren't planning on a resurrection. They were just going to redecorate the tomb.

We don't need to waste our time redecorating the tomb and dressing it up. We need to resurrect the dead man on the inside. God doesn't want to redecorate your life. Jesus didn't come to just repaint your problem. You can't just drop a church service on Sunday morning into your schedule and hope it changes everything.

God wants to walk into the lives of men who have died—men who are far away from Him—men who are bound with drugs, alcohol, pornography, sin, power, greed and ego, and He wants to resurrect you. God wants to take the limits off you and radically change who you are and where you've been.

There is a powerful movement emanating from heaven right now, and men are being born again. These men are not just turning into church members and attendees. They are men who have met the living God—men who are free on the inside—men who once were lost but now are found.

> God wants to take the limits off you and radically change who you are and where you've been.

Upon arriving in Bethany Jesus told Martha that He was the resurrection and the life. Jesus is the author of resurrection and restoration. He is the firstfruits of all those who will follow His victory and discover the power of His resurrection in their own lives.

I call this second chance at life that only Jesus can create a bounce back. Jesus' resurrection from the power of death, hell and the grave is the greatest comeback of all time. His comeback became the open door for your bounce back!

Left to ourselves we all fall.

> *For all have sinned and fall short of the glory of God.*
>
> *Romans 3:23*

Everyone falls, but not everyone gets up. Far too many of our brothers have fallen, and they can't get up. They have listened to the mourners and have believed they were created to fall, so for them the battle is over before it ever began.

Jesus Himself had some rough days as He walked this earth in our skin on His way to our cross. He had some hard knocks. He was unjustly judged. He was unfairly condemned. He was unbelievably betrayed. He was undeservedly abandoned by those closest to Him. He was unthinkably beaten and tortured. He was unspeakably crucified, yet unforced. He allowed it all for the sake of our salvation.

He bounced back and, with Him, so can you.

> *And if the Spirit of him who raised Jesus from the dead is living in you, he who raised Christ from the dead will also give life to your mortal bodies through his Spirit, who lives in you.*
>
> *Romans 8:11*

Jesus Christ was raised from the dead by the power of the Holy Spirit. In looking at Romans 8:11, not only do we discover that Jesus was raised from the dead by the power of the Holy Spirit but we also encounter the incredible truth that this same Spirit comes to live in us when Jesus Christ becomes our Savior. That means the Spirit of resurrection, the Spirit of the "bounce back" is now in us! We can get up and try again. It's not over.

> Resurrection removes all your previous limitations. It releases a new season, a new paradigm, a new man.

Some may never turn to Christ until they hit bottom. If you feel as if you've hit rock bottom in your life, be encouraged. You're in the right place to begin a bounce back! Like a rubber ball falling under the force of gravity, as you strike the floor you can shift the momentum of your life back into an upward direction. But you must realize that you can only change direction when Jesus Christ has entered your life. Otherwise you may fall to the ground and splatter from the force of your fall like an egg.

Everyone falls but not everyone gets up. Choose to change direction and get back up through the power of the Holy Spirit today.

In his blind fury to destroy your authentic manhood, there is one fatal concept Satan did not take into account. In his attempt to destroy you, he may have forcefully thrown you to the ground but, similar to a rubber ball, the harder the fall the higher the bounce back. With Christ, your bounce back becomes greater than your fall! That's the power of the Holy Spirit's restoration. You're not Humpty Dumpty and God is not scrambling madly around trying to put you back together again. You can bounce back. You can be restored to be better than you were before your fall!

Resurrection removes all your previous limitations. It releases a new season, a new paradigm, a new man.

Today a Lazarus generation of authentic men is being resurrected by the word of Almighty God and the power of the Holy Spirit.

These men aren't going to settle for dead religion. They've already been dead. They've already been in the tomb. They don't want to come into a church building and sit around in another one. They aren't interested in being around men who talk the talk but don't walk the walk. They are tired of going through the motions with no life inside.

These men are being resurrected by the power of God, and they are becoming FivestarMen, positioned by God to change their lives and their world.

CHAPTER EIGHT
CAN THESE BONES LIVE?

"Lazarus, come out!"

One simple statement. Three short words. That's all that is needed when God's Word is spoken in His authority and by the power of the Holy Spirit. Jesus cried in a loud voice, "Lazarus, come out!" and the dead man came out.

The voice of God is speaking to men in America. God is calling to us, saying, "Men of God, rise up!" We are poised to move the stone out of the way. We are ready to change the culture. God is going to resurrect authentic manhood, and we will stand as an army, marching side by side together to do the glorious works of God.

When God's timing and God's will come together, and He can find someone to declare His Word in that moment, nothing can restrain His purpose, not even death.

*The hand of the L*ORD *was on me, and he brought me out by the Spirit of the L*ORD *and set me in the middle of a valley; it was full of bones. He led me back and forth among them, and I saw a great many bones on the floor of the valley, bones that were very dry. He asked me, "Son of man, can these bones live?" I said, "Sovereign L*ORD*, you alone know." Then he said to me, "Prophesy to these bones and say to them, 'Dry bones, hear the word of the L*ORD*! This is what the Sovereign L*ORD *says to these bones: I will make breath enter you, and you will come to life. I will attach tendons to you and make flesh come upon you and cover you with skin; I will put breath in you, and you will come to life. Then you will know that I am the L*ORD*.'"*

Ezekiel 37:1–6

"Son of man, can these bones live?"

The prophet said that the task was so great, only God knew the answer.

You may not feel strong. You may not feel that you can launch a movement that will do such work. But all God is asking you to do is speak the words that He gives you and stand up and represent Him.

Every flood began with one drop of rain. Every raging fire began with one small spark. Every revival began with one sincere prayer of repentance. Every movement that ever changed the world began with one person.

What you do matters.

One morning a man was jogging along the beach. As he reached a certain location, he discovered that a rare phenomenon had occurred the night before and tens of thousands of starfish had been washed up on shore. As the tide receded, these creatures were left behind to slowly die in the sun. The man was saddened to think

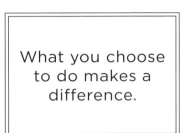

What you choose to do makes a difference.

about the inevitable fate of all the starfish, but there were so many. What could he do?

As the man continued his jog he met a young boy. The boy was walking along the beach, throwing the starfish back into the ocean. The man stopped for a moment as he realized what the boy was attempting to do. He told the boy that he should just give up, that there was no way he could possibly save all the starfish by himself. He asked, "What difference could you possibly make?"

The boy looked at the single starfish he held in his hand and replied, "To him, it makes all the difference in the world," and he threw the creature back into the sea.

What you choose to do makes a difference.

You may think, "It's too late for me. I've gone too far. I've made too many mistakes. I'm done."

The mess we may have made of our lives does not intimidate Jesus. There is no sin greater than the power of the cross. There is no one beyond the reach of God's unending grace and mercy.

Even Lazarus's sisters did not want to roll the stone away from his tomb. They were afraid the stench of death would be overwhelming and embarrassing.

But God is going to walk up to the tomb of men no one wanted to talk to, look at, or think about anymore and bring them back to vitality with His resurrection power.

God is interjecting a new voice of hope into the crypt of fallen manhood. Like the clear, strong voice of Jesus at the tomb of Lazarus, God is sending forth a powerful sound in the midst of the dry scattered bones of our expired brothers. This is the voice of the Holy Spirit, the voice of unlimited resurrection life.

God will use every man who is willing. The hand of Almighty God is upon us. While everyone else is walking away from the tomb in defeat and despair, we are doing what we can with what we have where we are. God is placing His Word in our mouths and His Spirit on our lives. We're declaring hope and life in the midst of a vast graveyard of slain men and something is beginning to happen. We are ordinary men representing an extraordinary God. One by one our voices are beginning to combine together. The noise of the mourners is about to be drowned out by the sound of a new army of men who have been raised to life.

When the angel delivered God's message to Mary that she would give birth to the Messiah she was of stunned. "How?" she questioned. "I'm a virgin, engaged but not married."

The angel's reply gives us insight into how God releases heaven's will into earth's reality. The answer for Mary, for you, for me, for fallen men, and for everyone who needs help beyond themselves was given:

> *The Holy Spirit will come upon you, and the power*
> *of the Highest will overshadow you. . . . For with*
> *God nothing will be impossible.*

> *Luke 1:35, 37 NKJV*

There you have it. No matter how desperate and final a situation may appear, when the overshadowing presence and power of God are present, nothing is impossible.

Genesis 1:2 tells us, "The earth was formless and empty, darkness was over the surface of the deep," but in the very midst of this condition we are also told, "The Spirit of God was hovering over the waters." This was God's ordained moment to create, to change the status quo. The Spirit of God overshadowed the moment and the circumstances. His power was present to perform His will. Nothing would be impossible. God spoke, and everything came to life.

> We are ordinary men representing an extraordinary God.

This is still God's divine pattern today. Under the anointing of the Holy Spirit, God's spoken Word releases God's power to save, to heal, to create, and to resurrect a generation of buried men.

This generation is in need of authentic men—men of God who are going to walk up to the graveside of dead men and challenge them to rise up and walk in resurrection power. We're going to stand in the power of Almighty God. We're going to walk upon high places and speak to the dead the way the prophet Ezekiel did. We're going to begin to prophesy—to speak in the authority of the Word of God—and dead bones are going to come to life.

And as we live our lives connected to the Source of Life, the wind of the Spirit will blow on the dead bones of this generation and turn the valley of death into a valley of an innumerable army of living, breathing, authentic men of God.

CHAPTER NINE

GRAVE CLOTHES— HOW WILL THE CHURCH RESPOND?

*The dead man came out, his hands and feet
wrapped with strips of linen, and a cloth around his
face. Jesus said to them, "Take off the grave clothes
and let him go."*

John 11:44

The unbelievable happened! Lazarus came out of the grave resurrected to a new life and given a supernatural second chance. As he exited the tomb, it was apparent that his mobility was severely limited. His hands and feet were still wrapped with strips of linen and a cloth was tied around his face.

Jesus had done His part, and then He told the concerned family and friends that it was their turn to team up with Him in the resurrected transformation of Lazarus. Jesus told the people at the tomb, "You take off the grave clothes and let Lazarus go."

Graves are going to open and men from all over this world are going to be resurrected. God is going to send men new spirits and new identities. God is going to raise up genuine, God-designed manhood in this day. We're going to see the dead come to life. Jesus is raising them from the dead, and we are charged to help them get out of their old, filthy grave clothes.

Men are going to start coming out of their tombs and walking into our churches. The odds are high that they may be quite different from our accepted norms. They may dress inappropriately. They might not know how to act. They might smell as if they've been dead for a long time. They might do and say things that are embarrassing. To be

> Men are going to start coming out of their tombs and walking into our churches.

sure, they won't come right out of a prayer closet. They might come right out of the grave, the bar, or the boardroom.

I'm reminded of a minister friend who recounted a "grave clothes" story in a recent conversation. He told of an incident that occurred during a prayer service. The evangelist was attempting to pray for an unusually large number of people. He became concerned that people had to wait for a long time to share their requests and receive prayer. Trying to speed up the process, he ill advisedly turned to an unfamiliar man standing nearby and told him with his best "Christianese" language to "curse the cancer" that had invaded an elderly woman's body. You can guess what happened next. The brand-new Christian, in his most sincere concern for the lady gave the illness a thorough cussing out (*%##@*%)!

Sometimes removing grave clothes can be messy. Help remove them anyway.

These men have been in hell. Satan has been stealing, killing, and destroying them and they're not going to come out of the grave perfected. They will be stumbling over the old clothes that have entangled them. Their hearts will be changed, but they won't know how to untangle themselves from their filthy rags of bondage.

What do the grave clothes represent?

They are the residual trappings of death, the reminders of a failed life before Christ rescued them. These men are forgiven and accepted by God. His Spirit now indwells them, but that old nature—the carnal nature—still remains, trying its best to keep them wrapped up and limited.

As we find in the parable of the sower in Matthew 13, if the enemy cannot stop them from receiving God's Word, he will endeavor to limit the impact of the new life they have received. He will attempt to choke their potential and their fruitfulness with the grave clothes of the cares and weights of life.

Their grave clothes are the wounds, hurts, and hang ups they carry from their past life on the other side of the tombstone. It is the baggage they laboriously drag from the dysfunction they grew up in and the heartache inflicted from broken promises and failed dreams. Many carry the weight of guilt and shame from their own mistakes. These newly resurrected men are going to need some help to walk out their new calling in Christ.

> *You were taught, with regard to your former way of life, to put off your old self, which is being corrupted by its deceitful desires; to be made new in the attitude of your minds; and to put on the new self, created to be like God in true righteousness and holiness.*
>
> *Ephesians 4:22–24*

We must first put off something old before we can put on something new.

In Lazarus's day, the most binding of all agreements that were entered into were covenants. One of the most important steps in the process of a covenant agreement was the exchanging of robes. In that culture your robe signified your identity. You could look at a man's robe and immediately discern his status in society and know who his family was. When two men exchanged robes with each other in a covenant, they were making an incredibly powerful statement. They were declaring from that day forward their names and their identities were irrevocably connected.

> *I delight greatly in the LORD; my soul rejoices in my God. For he has clothed me with garments of salvation and arrayed me in a robe of his righteousness.*
>
> *Isaiah 61:10*

As new men with new lives in Christ, we have put off our old identities and put on the original redeemed identities that God designed for us while we were still in our mothers' wombs. In exchange for our grave clothes, we have been clothed with garments of salvation and arrayed in the robe of His righteousness. This is the great exchange.

It is our responsibility to help this newly resurrected army of men live free and unencumbered from their grave clothes. This is the real ongoing work of the church.

The term we use for this process of taking off the old and putting on the new is *discipleship*. Jesus commanded His church to share the gospel with everyone on this planet and to make disciples of everyone who receives the good news.

At this juncture the church must ask itself a very probing question. Do we truly desire to partner with God in this great resurrection movement of authentic manhood? Meaning: Will we wholeheartedly commit our time and resources to every man God brings our way?

All men everywhere? Or just the ones who look like us, talk like us, and live like us? (You know, the ones who can help our church.) What about those who need our help?

> In exchange for our grave clothes, we have been clothed with garments of salvation and arrayed in the robe of His righteousness.

What about those who wear different "robes" than our familiar church family and don't fit into our demographics? Will men from different racial groups, divergent socio-economic classes, varying theological environments, and unchurched backgrounds be welcomed in our pews?

I believe that this concern of dealing with new believers and their issues may be the reason many churches are so indifferent toward true outreach and evangelism. They have smelled the stench of grave clothes before, and they're simply not willing to dirty their hands. Grave clothes can be extremely pungent and embedded in rotten flesh at times. It requires painstaking, unselfishly dedicated labor to remove them.

In the book of Ezekiel we read about the bones of dead men coming together as God's Spirit breathed life into them. In Ezekiel 37:7, you will notice that as life flooded into the valley of dead and dry bones, chaos seemed to momentarily visit. As the wind blew, there was a great commotion and the bones began to rattle—but God was still completely in control.

This movement may be messy. To be sure, the resurrection of a new army of men will stretch us. But I believe the church will respond, and we will become stronger believers in the process.

> These men will not only need help in removing their old grave clothes, they will need our love and wisdom as they begin to put on their new identities.

How well do we know the Word of God? How is our prayer life lately? Are we willing to be true servant leaders? Are we reaching for a title or a towel? Is having power and control in our local churches what motivates us, or will we be willing to lay down our positions and titles for the sake of expanding God's kingdom?

Are we ready?

How will the church respond as authentic manhood is raised back to life by the power of the Holy Spirit?

God is willing to raise men from the dead and bring them in. He'll roll away the stone and bring them to life. But He has given you and me the responsibility to take their grave clothes off.

We have a part to play in their resurrection.

Are we going to love God and care about these men enough to take time to unwrap them?

Are we willing to devote our time to meet with these new converts and disciple them? Are we willing to answer the questions we think they should already have the answers to? Are we willing to open our hearts and develop genuine friendships with these men?

These new brothers will come from every spectrum of society.

Some will have been "down and out" and some will have been "up and out." Death is the same for every man no matter how much was paid for his casket.

These men will not only need help in removing their old grave clothes, they will need our love and wisdom as they begin to put on their new identities. These men have been redeemed from hell. They will not be content to just sit on a pew.

They must be taught to trust and obey the Word of God. They must be shown how to build a devotional lifestyle and how to walk with God. They must be led to understand the new nature they have received through Christ. We must help them find and develop the gifts and abilities God has placed inside them and show them the importance of serving the purposes of God with their unique giftings.

We owe these new brothers the accurate teaching of God's Word, explaining that how they conduct themselves at work is just as important as how they worship in a church building. They need to know a Christian's life is not divided between the sacred and secular. Every day is holy and wholly given over to God. They need to be coached in the idea that their work is a fundamental element of their witness.

If we really believe men in the church need to lead, and fathers need to train the next generation, we will commit ourselves to becoming the teachers, mentors, and leaders God has called us to become.

> *Jesus said, "If you hold to my teaching, you are really my disciples. Then you will know the truth, and the truth will set you free."*
>
> *John 8:31, 32 (author's paraphrase)*

Lately, many in the church have developed the world's philosophies, *"I'm okay. You're okay"* and *"If it feels good do it."* Men have swallowed the Kool-Aid of this particular generation and accepted the faulty reasoning, *"Who am I to say what's right or wrong?"*

In far too many churches today the predominant fragrance is grave clothes—not new grave clothes that are being removed but old grave clothes. No one is changing. People have been introduced to Christ but not to discipleship. We're supposed to be moving from glory to glory and faith to faith (2 Corinthians 3:18, Romans 1:17).

The process is further described in God's Word.

> *Now thanks be to God who always leads us in triumph in Christ, and through us diffuses the fragrance of His knowledge in every place.*
>
> *2 Corinthians 2:14 NKJV*

As mature believers we must stop compromising and tell the truth in love. We must proclaim that the resurrection power of Christ is greater than any bonds of death that may still be clinging to these new converts. Men can come as they are and leave as He is!

We cannot hold back and let these men stay the way they are because we don't want to get dirty. Only the truth will set these men free. Real friends will tell you the truth.

It's not about what you or I say. It's about what God says. We're not making the rules. We're just the men carrying the mail. We need to walk in the love of Christ and have confidence that if we tell the truth, God will set people free.

CHAPTER TEN

HOW WILL YOU RESPOND?

God cared about you when everyone else had given up. God saved you when no one else would even talk to you. God delivered you from addictions, habits, and life-controlling bondages that you could never break in a thousand years. Some of these sins and habits were hidden from your family and your friends. You had been leading a double life. What started as a game, a flirtation, a "pet sin" had become your master, and it was only a matter of time before everything in your world was about to crash and burn along with you. If you had a million dollars to pay the greatest psychiatrist in the world and could lie on his leather couch for twenty-four hours a day, he could not take out of you what the Devil put in you.

But then you had one moment in the presence of Almighty God. Jesus walked into your life and released you from the sin that had run through your veins for generations.

I ask you, the recipient of resurrection, how will you respond?

Will you respond with gratitude?

The Bible says he who has been forgiven of much should love much (Luke 12:48). When you've experienced grace, like the woman caught in the act of adultery, Jesus says to you, "Go and sin no more" (John 8:11).

You've been released and set free. Now it's your move.

It's time for you to move forward in your relationship with God.

> It's your turn to decide if you are going to follow Jesus wholeheartedly.

You were comparable to the lame man at the Gate Beautiful. Before you met the power of God, your friends had to carry you around on a mat, but once you met Jesus, you didn't need anyone to carry you. You just needed someone to help you learn how to walk in the right direction because you were headed somewhere new. You're no longer the man who was lame. In fact the only name we find for that man in the Bible was, "a man crippled from birth" (Acts 3:1–10).

But you have a new identity. Now you are the man who was healed. You have a new reason to live. It's your turn to respond. It's your turn to decide how you're going to walk. It's your turn to decide if you are going to follow Jesus wholeheartedly.

I believe that you will.

In Mark 10:46–52, we meet a blind man named Bartimaeus. He heard that Jesus would pass by the very place where he daily begged for alms. He knew this was his only chance to be set free from his burden. No one else could help him. It was Jesus or nothing. All or none. As Jesus drew closer, Bartimaeus went all out. He began to yell at the top of his voice. Everyone tried to quiet him down, but no one mattered to him but Jesus.

As He always does, Jesus responded to a desperate man's faith. Jesus stopped and called Bartimaeus to come to Him. What happened next is a lesson that everyone must learn.

> *Throwing his cloak aside, he jumped to his feet and came to Jesus.*
>
> *Mark 10:50*

As Bartimaeus jumped to his feet he threw his cloak aside. What could be the importance of that gesture?

Everything! His cloak was his license to beg. Only those recognized by the government were allowed to beg on the streets. The cloak Bartimaeus wore was his identity and his only means of survival. When the Master called him—even before he was healed—Bartimaeus threw away every connection with his past life and totally trusted Jesus. There would be no going back.

That's exactly how you should respond today.

> *Then Jesus said, "Did I not tell you that if you believed, you would see the glory of God?" So they took away the stone. Then Jesus looked up and said, "Father, I thank you that you have heard me. I knew that you always hear me, but I said this for the benefit of the people standing here, that they may believe that you sent me." When he had said this, Jesus called in a loud voice, "Lazarus, come out!" The dead man came out, his hands and feet wrapped with strips of linen, and a cloth around his*

face. Jesus said to them, "Take off the grave clothes and let him go." Therefore many of the Jews who had come to visit Mary, and had seen what Jesus did, put their faith in him. But some of them went to the Pharisees and told them what Jesus had done.

John 11:40–46

When he was raised from the dead, Lazarus was given a brand new identity. That resurrection not only changed his life, but it also revolutionized the ministry of Jesus. The impact of the resurrection of Lazarus brought people to a point of decision—either they were going to believe in Jesus or they were not.

> When God begins to resurrect dead men and authentic manhood, it changes cities. It changes churches. It changes families.

Some people said, "Now we're going to have to kill Jesus. That man's raising the dead, and His days are numbered."

They should have known better. How do you kill a man who just killed death? There were hundreds of people standing on the sidelines who witnessed the resurrection power of God and they had to make a decision. Is Jesus the Son of God or not? Is Jesus who He says He is or not? Many believed because of the miracle they saw.

The resurrection of Lazarus changed the whole region. What God has done for you has the power to help everyone around you get a fresh perspective of Jesus.

I've seen this dozens of times, yet it never becomes commonplace. In the last few months a man who once attended our church as a young adult has come home. He not only moved away from our city years ago, he moved away from his God. In the midst of professional success he faced the sting of a very personal loss—the loss of his marriage. In this moment of heartache and disappointment he has come back to faith in Christ. He has been resurrected. In the short space of a few weeks, his teenage children have all followed their father to Christ.

I've witnessed the power of a resurrected man's influence again and again. There are very few dynamics that are this compelling. These men literally become open doors for the healing and grace of God to wonderfully invade the most hopeless of situations.

As the message went into Jerusalem and the people saw Lazarus walking around raised from the dead, even the priests began to believe. The city was shaken.

When God begins to resurrect dead men and authentic manhood, it changes cities. It changes churches. It changes families. It changes individuals.

The resurrection of authentic manhood will blow across the hearts of men who've become preoccupied, men who've become indifferent, and men who've lost their way. It will change the hearts of men who have lost their identities and disconnected from the creation and purpose of God for their lives.

God is speaking to men everywhere that it's time for resurrection.

God is speaking to you.

Are you connected to God? Are you where you need to be? Are you dying, sick, and infirmed because you're separated from His presence? Have you lived dangerously close to death for so long you've assumed that's how it has to be?

Has your love for God been so watered down that you haven't

sensed His presence for many months? Do you pray anymore? Do you love people anymore?

No matter where you find yourself today, God is not through with you yet.

God is going to take the message of the resurrection of authentic manhood and start something brand new in your life.

Perhaps you have been a prodigal. You left the Father's house, the place where you belong. Maybe you grew up in church, and you know the gospel of Jesus Christ, but somewhere you got off track. You took your possessions and went out and had a good time for a season, but you began to waste away because you were separated from the

> God is going to take the message of the resurrection of authentic manhood and start something brand new in your life.

Father. You were separated from His presence for so long that your faith and your hope finally died. You thought you'd never come back—but every day the Father has been looking for you to return.

Today is your day. This is your moment. You've been lying in a pigpen, living in a tomb. You know if you don't do something quickly, you're going to die

Come home.

The Father will jump off the front porch, grab and hug you, and say, "Let's celebrate! My son is back!"

Your coat and shoes are still sitting there. They are yours alone. They don't fit anyone else. Your ring is there ready for you to pick it up and put it back on. It is your ring that was made for your finger.

Every plan that God ever had for you—every purpose He ever designed for you—every gift He ever put in your life—it's not dead, it's just waiting for you to come back home. If you let yourself die, no one else can wear your shoes. No one else can wear your ring, or your robe. You will leave a void.

Your wife will miss you. Your children will miss you. The church will miss you. Society will miss you.

Your destiny awaits.

All you have to do in this moment is say, "Spirit of the living God, raise me back to life. Come sweep into this tomb. Come pull me out of this pigpen. Restore me to life one more time."

This is your moment.

Respond and be resurrected.

PRAYERS

As you have read this message of hope and resurrection you have come to realize that this is no coincidence. God has spoken to you through the pages of this book. Something is stirring deep within your heart that you have never understood before. The search you have been on all your life finally has a name. That name is Jesus. At this very moment you recognize that it is His voice calling to you from outside your tomb. Pray this prayer now, and your new life will begin.

A prayer for those coming to Christ for the first time:

Dear Jesus, I come to You today, and I need Your help. I need to begin a new life. I realize only You can give me this second chance. I believe that You are God's Son. I believe that You died on the cross in my place. Today, right now, I ask You to forgive me of my sins and to come live in my heart. I give You all my life—all the good and all the bad. I'm Yours. Please exchange my weakness for Your strength and my death for Your life. I confess that You are now my Savior and my Lord. Thank You, Jesus. In Your name, I pray. Amen.

A prayer for those who have walked away from their relationship with Christ and are ready to recommit themselves to Him:

Dear Jesus, I'm the prodigal son. I took Your presence in my life for granted, and I've strayed so far away. I've wondered if it was too late for me. I've wondered if I could ever find my way back to You. I'm so thankful that I have found Your grace and mercy again. Today I repent of my sins. Please forgive me and take me back. I surrender everything to You, and I receive Your life and Spirit. My life begins anew here and now. In Your name, I pray. Amen.

ABOUT THE AUTHOR
GEORGE SAWYER

George Sawyer is the founding pastor of Calvary Assembly in Decatur, Alabama. From a small beginning in a rented storefront property, it now has more than 2,000 people in attendance each week at three campuses, including the Decatur Dream Center and a residential women's drug and alcohol recovery ministry. Calvary is on the cutting edge of what God is doing worldwide. Pastor Sawyer has led the church to become a model of a completely multi-ethnic congregation whose many outreach ministries influence every level of society in the state. A recipient of the prestigious Lilly Foundation Award, Calvary Assembly has distinguished itself as one of the top-300 Protestant churches in America.

George Sawyer is a revolutionary communicator who inspires passion and excellence by effectively applying the Word of God to everyday life. His messages are broadcast weekly on network television in the state. A sought-after speaker, George speaks in numerous domestic and international training conferences and has ministered in more than twenty countries around the globe. He lives his life without limits. George and his wife, Phyllis, enjoy living in Decatur, Alabama, with their two married daughters and their families and the great people who make up their wonderful church family.

CONTACT INFORMATION

To contact the author or to obtain more information

Please Contact:

George Sawyer

Calvary Assembly

1413 Glenn St SW

Decatur, AL 35603

256-355-7440

pastor@calvaryassembly.org

To obtain information on

hosting a FivestarMan Event, visit:

FivestarMan.com

★ ★ ★ ★ ★

Please include your testimony of how this book has helped you
when you write. Prayer requests are welcome.

To order more copies of this book visit www.myhealthychurch.com